Made in the USA
Monee, IL
12 May 2021

68451875R00056